D1252773

Flare

poems by

Camisha L. Jones

Finishing Line Press
Georgetown, Kentucky

Flare

ACKNOWLEDGMENTS

Some poems included in this book have been previously published. "What the
Deafened Girl Hears" and "The Law of Motion" are published in *Cape Cod Poetry
Review*. "Accommodation," an earlier version of "In/Ability," and "Praise Song
for the Body" were first published in *The Deaf Poets Society* inaugural issue. "On
Having an Autoimmune Disease," "Ménière's Flare," and "Wrecking Ball" were first
published in *Typo*, guest edited by Jennifer Bartlett. "Acoustics Test," "Tinnitus,"
and "The Sound Barrier" (in an earlier version) are included in the *Unfolding the
Soul of Black Deaf Expressions* exhibit book. "Ode to the Chronically Ill Body" was
first published online by Split This Rock in *The Quarry: A Social Justice Poetry
Database* and as part of their Poem of the Week series.

Publisher: Leah Maines

Editor: Christen Kincaid

Cover Art: Robalú Gibsun, robartistic.weebly.com

Author Photo: Brandon T. Woods, www.bwoodsphotography.com

Cover Design: Elizabeth Maines McCleavy

Printed in the USA on acid-free paper.
Order online: www.finishinglinepress.com
        also available on amazon.com

Author inquiries and mail orders:
Finishing Line Press
P. O. Box 1626
Georgetown, Kentucky 40324
U. S. A.

Table of Contents

Intercession 1

Ode to the Chronically Ill Body 3

The Law of Motion 5

Haunted 7

Fibromyalgia: A Haiku 9

Wrecking Ball 10

My Anxieties Learn to Pray 11

The Sound Barrier 13

Scars 14

Accommodation 15

Tinnitus 16

What the Deafened Girl Hears 17

Acoustics Test 18

Ménière's Flare 20

In/Ability 21

Ode to My Hearing Aids 23

When the Doctor Says Lupus 24

On Having an Autoimmune Disease 25

On Loss 26

Flare 27

Praise Song for the Body 28

Intercession

when I confess the pain
they tell me of a glad morning
they say I come out of this
with a long awaited joy

> *still I become*
> *a fiery tongue*
> *to scorch the earth*
> *the bluest flame*
> *licking each muscle and joint*

they send their prayers
cover me with expectations

> *how to forgive the body of its many sins*
> *how to forgive what's already*
> *on its knees unrepentant*

they say I am healed
they say it is already done

> *I come out*
> *I scorch the earth*
> *I leave only ash*

If I pray I come out of this, they say
My hands learn not to flick the lighter
My bones unlearn the taste for char

> *I forgive   I pray*
> *I scorch this earth*
> *Become one with its combustion*

If I wait, they say, my change will come

I am the fire
I am the smoke

I strike the match
I strike the match

Ode to the Chronically Ill Body

This body is   one long moan

    My feet   a landscape of mines
    My legs   two full pails of water I spill
                             at the weight of
    My back   where the sharpest knives are kept
    My hands   a scatter of matches   ready to spark into flame

This body   is lightning
  Strikes the same place   more than twice

This body   is a fist   pounding its own hand
This body   crumples like paper
    I crumple   like paper   because of this body
This body   just wants   and wants   and wants
This body
        Says stop
  Says go
        Says stop
  Says run
        Says stop
        Says STOP
This body is   a stubborn traffic light   stuck on red
This body will
        have what it wants   Or it is
           blasphemous   tantrum down every grocery store aisle
This body   makes an embarrassment   of me

This body is
   an embarrassment
         Then pleasure   Then hunger
               Then defender   Then defendant
         Then carriage
               Then coffin
This body is   Tupperware with its secrets   sealed tight
This body   scrapes   and falls
Then gets back up   again   and again
         It's all I got   to get back up with   again
This body   is an ocean   of oil spill   all over me.

The Law of Motion

A body in motion tends to stay in motion
Til it is compelled to do otherwise.
—Isaac Newton's First Law of Motion

the day your body
hugs the fender
of an oncoming car
you learn physics

you learn what it takes
to convince a body
to take flight

you glide through air
without resistance
without knowing you could

then
                    fall
then crash
then become immobile

and survive

but you don't forget
the moment between
standing upright and landing on flat dirt

you keep that memory

you remember
all that scattered to the ground
the balancing act
the firm grip
the ridiculous notion that you ever had any control

and when your mother dies
when your grandmother has the stroke
when there is something beneath the skin they think might kill
you remember the crash

the sudden impact
the unexpected need for repair
the places compelled to turn tender & scar

how familiar it all feels
to be undone by reality
speeding too fast
between 6 lanes
of life's constant motion
bruising the bones of every certainty you hold

it all scatters to the ground
tells you we are fragile beings
bent on dying
some day
before we think it's time

this life
is a moving vehicle
heading straight towards the thing
that will finish us

sometimes
we just think it will finish us
and that's the thing
that does

Haunted

I dream of pebbles under my pillow
and wake with their imprints.

The pests that live within my walls
eat at me. I pry their tiny mouths open,
inspect their teeth.

I am a land of pebbles and pests.
Something always scampering
under my clothes, agitating
in my shoe.

I do all the math.
Counting on catastrophe,
Multiplying the "What Ifs."
I am the equation I still can't solve.

I never wanted a bike or a car.
Still, too often I am a lawn
full of things with wheels
that go nowhere:
unsightly and immobile.

Sometimes I worry about this property's value.

I am a tug of war, the distance
between choices and their consequences
pulling me like a rope.

When people try to love me
and my heart loves them back,
I become detective, daily
obsessing over the hows and whens
of their inevitable deaths.

I take note of potholes,
plant my anxieties on them
as safety cones. Let them turn
orange and ripe enough to stew in.
To my beloveds, I offer these
as tonic. They sip & complain of its bitter.

I've never liked Halloween,
welcoming the horror, dressing up
to shock and scare. Nevertheless,
inside my fear, there I am everyday:
adorned in fangs, at my own door,
knocking.

Fibromyalgia: A Haiku

Me and body think
Different. Argue fiercely.
Call each other sick.

Wrecking Ball

sometimes work
is a wrecking ball

makes me a high rise
with good reason to crumble

sometimes play
turns me to kindling

kissed by my own flame
burned into ash

I push the boulder
of this body uphill

just to pick up the mail

turn into tortoise
trapped in the rigid shell
of *you look so healthy*

how incredible   this body
as it summits into speed bumps
into fog and pulse and bruise

magnificent in its invisible injury

My Anxieties Learn to Pray

They refuse to bend their knees
Instead they hide their faces
Fill their twisted mouths with lament
An arrogant language of the hopeless

They refuse to say "thank you"
Say the words are hot coals in their desert mouths

They don't believe in God   or rescue
They believe   one regular day at the metro
Someone will be pushed off the platform
They suspect it will be me
They suspect my hands might want to do the pushing

They don't believe in grace
They believe in busy   running
Me around on the leash of their sovereignty

They believe in the automobile's ability to accident
The graceful spin of one object
Crashing unexpectedly into another

They believe in caution
Staying in the house on a sunny day
Just in case it rains

They believe in the rain
Put all their faith in it
Like the fastest horse at the race

They believe in time running out
Curtains opening too soon
On the delicious punch line that is me

They refuse to bow their knees
Or bend their reasons
Or break their promises

But when I clasp my hands
They clasp theirs too
When I close my eyes
Throw my wishes into the well of the Infinite
Their chant   for a moment
becomes still as a whisper

The Sound Barrier

Exactly 2
That's the number of times most people tolerate being asked:
"Could you repeat that?"

Then conversations come to an abrupt halt like a telephone line gone dead.
No one likes being hung up on so I pretend to hear when I don't.
I shake my head "yes" when the answer should be "huh!?"

Being hard of hearing is kinda like filling in the blanks
of a Wheel of Fortune puzzle.

Ca__ You U_dersta__ __ The Wor__s Comi__g Out M__ Mouth?
My ears are constantly tuned to a station with a weak signal.
Broken radios are considered throw-away items so I hide my "affliction."
It wasn't always this way.
At first, I tried different techniques.
I asked for specifics: "Could you repeat the last **three** words?"
I gave instructions: "It helps if you enunciate and pause between the words."
And when that didn't work, I asked "Can you *just* write it down?"
I glanced at the pen and paper pushed back at me,
        the backs of those who hear well as they walked away
        and wondered to myself what seemed so unreasonable
        about exerting half the effort I did.

I have a memory.
It is of walking down the street with a friend.
He is on my right and we are talking.
He places his hands at my waist
        and they guide me to the right. He shifts to my left.
He knows I hear better that way.
When I still don't understand what's said,
        he repeats himself a 3rd time.

It isn't just the words I hear.
It is in moments like these that I know
        even with these "defective" ears,
I'm able to hear everything that's really important.

Scars

Blessed be the scar on my right knee,
the territory it claims as landmark,
preserving the day this body
plus that car didn't mean dying.

Blessed be the body
knowing to get back up
from the ground when it can.

Blessed be the scarred geography
of my left arm,
the mapped history
of intimate touch with irons,
so much popped oil,
the warm insides of that one stove.

Blessed be all that teaches what can happen
between flame and refusing to see what's there.

Blessed be the scar in the lowest valley of my back,
the red wagon I was never supposed to be in,
the swift pull of someone else's hand.

Blessed be my mother's warning,
my foolish disobedience.
Praise for now knowing what's wise
from what speeds too fast for me.

Blessed be the scar swimming cross my right breast,
a fish-shaped wound from a battle
doctors never had to wage.

Blessed be their suspicion, their needles, the carving knife.
Blessed be the body trying to turn on itself
the relief of knowing it failed.

Accommodation

The law wants my body reasonable
My body won't fence in its demands
Expects the world to stop
Whenever it wants to lay down
Throws up its middle finger
At deadlines, task lists,
Long awaited meetings
It ain't open to negotiation
Wants you to stop telling it to
Calm down
It has three settings: rest, spark, flare
All that talk about your inconvenience & your hardship
It calls that *Bullshit*
It will not wait in line
It will not be polite
It will not use its inside voice
It wants all the space
In every room of the house
The entire sky & the full lawn of grass
It wants to set it all aflame
My body is a pyromaniac
My body is the art
Of Angela Bassett's right hand
Letting reason go up in smoke

Tinnitus

It comes on like a wave
crashing   riptide
pulling me under
with its strong hands

strangling sound
til each sentence becomes
a sidewalk   sliced into parts
that I can't cross

each statement   a shore
too far to reach

and people

just keep talking
their unknown tongue
like I am not being attacked
right before their eyes

like they've never seen
a woman   drowning

What the Deafened Girl Hears

a washing machine

> *Pray there is no spin cycle*
> *Pray to come out clean*
> *Pray. Rinse. Repeat.*

thunder in every drum

> *Pray there'll be no twister*
> *Pray the lightning flares but doesn't strike*

an entire ocean

> *Pray when the waves crash*
> *Pray over what the waves break*

a tunnel of echoes

> *Pray the walls won't close*
> *For light on the other side*

a persistent dial tone

> *Pray no one hangs up*
> *Hang on even when they hang up*

a test of the Emergency Broadcast System

> *Receive it all as a call to prayer*
> *Sit still & search for a God to listen*

Acoustics Test

Say the word "pan-cake"
pan-cake
Say the word "birth-day"
birth-day
Say the word, "base-ball"
base-ball

This is a test

It's me up at bat
An audiologist on the mound
Pitching words to me slow
So I can catch them

This is a test
Random as "it" may be
With no cause or cure, I am here
Because of what I can't hear

Say the word "play-ground"
As far as Ménière's Disease is concerned
I am all swings and sliding boards
Stuck on the merry-go-round of vertigo, hearing loss, ear noise

Say the word "door-knob"
I am as deaf as one most days
Entering conversations only to be lost in them
My hearing never turns or unlocks completely

Say the word "dead-bolt"
Hearing
The faculty or sense by which sound is perceived
I perceive sound as code I can't always break

Say the word "jail-house"
I got no way to escape these ringing ears
The clanging against the bars
Dividing me from comprehension, from community

I say the word "side-walk"
Watch the wet pavement of hearing loss
Swallowing the weight of my aspirations
Then I say the word "mail-man"
Wait for these tests to deliver
Something worth repeating
      A *life-boat*
      An *air-plane*
To save me from all this *set-back*

Say the word "mouse-trap"
Say that the cheese I keep chasing is inclusion
Say my life is a sitcom
And I'm scared to be caught acting
With the right lines in the wrong scene

What will critics say about me then

Will they say the word "use-less"
Or "bro-ken" or "mis-fit"

And I know these aren't nouns
But Ménière's has a way
Of stripping the noun out of "hu-man"
Reducing me   to lesser adjectives
Reducing me   to echo

Ménière's Flare

and just like that
a light goes out
a bulb blows
sound becomes shadow
each sentence a gang in a dark alley
at the wrong time of night

the doctors
document the decline in angles
flat terrain and steep slopes
a landslide of loss

silence   swallows   everything
enjoys the taste of my pride
keeps me on a strict diet of asking for help
of needing accommodation

the blare of the tv
becomes whisper to me
a foreshadowing of the silent movie

my life becomes

spectacle
a 3 ringed circus
too many eyes on me
as each act unfolds

i become

"special" and suspicious
a dim light
flickering

In/Ability

in the shower
the sound of water
is crisp as a
head of lettuce
split in two

then fading
in the morning
when the running sink
becomes a whisper
in someone else's ear

daily I enter and exit
this turnstile of
here/hear and not here/hear

press my way through
a downpour of sound
divorced from meaning

I stand between the words
a mediator
and sometimes a barrier

sometimes
there is sweet song
birds chirping
a tune with no lyrics
keeping me company
in the silence

which isn't really silent
or quiet
but static
& loud

coupling & uncoupling
with comprehension

the mouth of each syllable muffled

language is an ocean
of murky water

words sinking
into buried grains of sand

a tide coming
and going

calling me the shore
calling me thousands of particles
stretched wide

receiving what the waves bring
surviving what they take away

Ode to My Hearing Aids

Then God said
let there be sound
and divided the silence
wide enough for music
to be let in and it was a good groove

And God said
let there be overflow
sent sound in all directions
pin drops & children's laughter
phones ringing & plates clattering
and it was kind of good but too much at times

So God said
let there be volume control
let there be choice how loud life should be
and there came the power to fade
the voices, the annoyances, the noise
and that was mighty good for all the unnecessary drama

Then God said *let there be surprise, startle even*
at the bird's chirp, the ice maker,
the cabinet slammed shut
let there be delight
at the first calls in months
to father & best friend
and these were such good reasons for choking back tears
that God saw
the dark & the light
dangling brilliantly from each ear
and God whispered *amen*
then smiled when it was heard.

When the Doctor Says Lupus

when she hands you the diagnosis
you hold it   awkward
inconsolable   offspring
wailing in your arms
your body   an oblivious vessel
an unprepared parent
wondering what this
will grow up to be

On Having an Autoimmune Disease

I bring my own house down
I build and break with the same hands
There's nothing to show for my work
I inhabit a strange land between disagreeable borders
There is a monster in the closet of this skin
She is the spitting image of me
She has keys I didn't give her
She is an anarchist
She likes the ash fire makes of me
Loves when I smell of smoke
At night, she scrapes my bones together for warmth
Sends up signals when I cry SOS
She loves seeing me burn
To become the flood
That smothers the flames
I drown here
She is an undertow with the strongest hands

On Loss

a new grief blooms
in the garden
outside my window
the yard is full
so I pluck the blossoms
that meet me at the door
put them in a jar
over the sink
they color my home
in every shade
of cool & dark hue
hang their heavy heads
in all the light and shadow
          till death comes
to take them too
leaving me with only the stems
not knowing what to do
with the bodies

Flare

If you could see

       the spectacular s p e c t r u m   of pain

the sparks   when they fly

would light up   the w i d e dark sky ENTIRELY

a strange thing   of beauty

      in its grotesque distortions

Praise Song for the Body

Praise for the body that takes pain and names it survival. That drinks anguish without ruling it bitter. Contains the daggers of sickness and bends them into a good home, a shelter, an escape route. Call this body miracle. Call it sanctuary. Name its ghosts but refuse to believe it is haunted. Refuse to give up on hope and all of its helium, its elevating power to raise this weighted vessel into a thing of light.

SO MUCH GRATITUDE!

First, to God for sustaining me through flare ups and as I've found my way as a writer. To those who've transitioned from this earth but left a legacy of tenacity for me to follow—especially my mother Barbara Jones, my grandmothers, Juanita Hicks and Rosa Jones, my great aunt Delores Horsley, my papa Fred Hicks. To my dad, Stanley Jones, for every "I know that's right" as I've made some of the riskiest decisions of my life, for believing my potential limitless. To my husband, Anthony Amos, this book would not have come to be without your support, your sacrifices, your confidence in me. Thank you is not enough.

Thanks to all my family for their love, for helping me believe in me—especially my aunt Catherine Henry, my cousin Yolanda Giles, my aunt Shirley Jones. To Alicia Fisher, Kendra Townes, and Valeria Gentry, for keeping me grounded, aiming high, inspired. Ya'll are the best sisters this only child could have! To Kenyada Jones, Howard & Melanie Parrish, and Angelique Palmer for their extraordinary support.

Thanks to the poetry communities that have embraced me, connected me to other poets of witness, helped me stand in my power unafraid of my own voice: Slam Richmond, Verbs and Vibes, Split This Rock, The Watering Hole. To John S. Blake, for setting a first real-life example of the discipline, passion, study, and artistry it takes to be a socially engaged poet. To my Split This Rock colleagues—especially Sarah Browning who's feedback on this collection is so cherished, Simone Roberts, and Tiana Trutna (all who've worked closest to me through the worst health challenges)—thank you for trusting my abilities, even when hearing loss and chronic pain made me question them myself. Thank you for cheering me on as I've written these poems.

Thanks to Robalú Gibsun for lending his stunning artwork for *Flare*; to Finishing Line Press for publishing it; to Susan Scheid for helping me order the manuscript; to Sarah Browning, Jennifer Bartlett, and Danez Smith for their kind words for the back cover; and to all the publications that have shared my work.

To all who find these poems meaningful, I am grateful. Let's break more silence!

Truth is, there's not space enough to thank everyone who's given me roots and wings to write this book. If your name doesn't appear, know I see you.

In 2010, **Camisha L. Jones** left a full-time job at her alma mater, the University of Richmond, to focus on writing. She had no clue what that meant. Lucky for her, she discovered Slam Richmond where she fell further in love with the craft and performance of poetry. As an active part of the spoken word community in Virginia, she has competed at the 2013 National Poetry Slam and performed at statewide gatherings such as Virginia Festival of the Book and James River Writers conference. She and her husband Anthony Amos co-led Verbs and Vibes Open Mic series in Charlottesville, Virginia for three years through his company SKIES THE LIMIT Entertainment.

Camisha's poems can be found at *Button Poetry, Beltway Poetry Quarterly, Typo, The Deaf Poets Society, Rogue Agent, pluck!,* the Dyer Arts Center's *Unfolding the Soul of Black Deaf Expressions* exhibition book, and *The Quarry*, Split This Rock's online social justice poetry database. Her writing is often shaped by her experiences with Ménière's Disease and fibromyalgia, as well as her 16 years of work leading community service and anti-bias initiatives at non-profits and institutions of higher education. She is also published in *Urban Views Weekly* newspaper, *Let's Get Real: What People of Color Can't Say and Whites Won't Ask about Racism* (StirFry Seminars & Consulting, Inc., 2011), *Class Lives: Stories from Across Our Economic Divide* (ILR Press, 2014), and *The Day Tajon Got Shot* (Shout Mouse Press, 2017).

Camisha was awarded a 2017 Spoken Word Immersion Fellowship from The Loft Literary Center. She is Managing Director at Split This Rock, a national non-profit based in DC that cultivates, teaches, and celebrates poetry that bears witness to injustice and provokes social change.

CPSIA information can be obtained
at www.ICGtesting.com
Printed in the USA
LVHW092028100320
649601LV00007B/1036

9 781635 342819